CALIFORNIA MEXICAN-SPANISH
COOK BOOK

LECTOR HOUSE PUBLIC DOMAIN WORKS

CALIFORNIA MEXICAN-SPANISH COOK BOOK

BERTHA HAFFNER-GINGER

ISBN: 978-93-5614-575-7

Published: 1914

CALIFORNIA MEXICAN-SPANISH COOK BOOK

SELECTED MEXICAN AND SPANISH RECIPES

BY

BERTHA HAFFNER-GINGER

1914

Very Sincerely Yours.

Bertha Haffner-Ginger

This book is dedicated to my daughter, nicknamed Miss "Paprika" by our pupils. She has been my inspiration and devoted companion through all the years of my public life.

B. H. G.

TO MY READERS

An announcement that my lesson for the day would be Spanish dishes, invariably brought record-breaking crowds in any city in the United States, and a demand for recipes induced me to search for the best to be found.

My three years' stay in California has enabled me to learn how to prepare the very best dishes directly from the natives, both Mexican and Spanish.

It is not generally known that Spanish dishes as they are known in California are really Mexican Indian dishes. Bread made of corn, sauces of chile peppers, jerked beef, tortillas, enchiladas, etc., are unknown in Spain as native foods; though the majority of Spanish people in California are as devoted to peppery dishes as the Mexicans themselves, and as the Mexicans speak Spanish, the foods are commonly called Spanish dishes.

When made properly, there is great merit in this class of foods and I have endeavored to select the very best recipes, and have revised them into correct proportions and practical methods of preparation.

Many of the dishes are very delicious and will be found of great value for luncheon, entries, and a zest to various menus, and especially useful to those who desire to cater to the public. Please note the classification of sauces and dressings which eliminates a repetition of the same sauce in different dishes.

Wishing you as much pleasure in the preparation and serving of this collection of recipes as I have had in compiling them, I am,

Very sincerely yours,
BERTHA HAFFNER-GINGER.

CLASSIFICATION OF RECIPES

The mission of the Old Padres was to make life brighter for such as these

REGULAR SPANISH DINNER

60c

Including Table Claret

SOUP

SALAD

ENCHILADAS

CARNE CON CHILI

SPANISH BEANS

SPANISH RICE

FRUIT AND COFFEE

Special Spanish Dinner

$1.50 per plate

A California "Ramada" Cafe

LISTA DE LOS PLATOS
(TABLE D'HOTE)

Ensalada de Frijoles
[Pink Bean Salad]

Sopa de Papas
[Potato Soup]

Arroz a la Creole
[Rice, Spanish]

Enchiladas a la Brabo

Enpanadas de Ternera, Espagnol
[Veal Cutlet, Spanish]

Frijoles Con Carne
[Pink Beans with Cheese]

Dulce de Naranja
[Orange Pudding]

Queso   **Galletas**
[Cheese]   [Crackers]

Cafe Negro
[Black Coffee]

DINNER, 75 Cents

LISTA DE LOS PLATOS
(TABLE D'HOTE)

Ensalada de Frijoles
[Pink Bean Salad]

Sopa de Papas
[Potato Soup]

Arroz a la Creole
[Rice, Spanish]

Enchiladas a la Brabo

Enpanadas de Ternera, Espagnol
[Veal Cutlet, Spanish]

Frijoles Con Carne
[Pink Beans with Cheese]

Dulce de Naranja
[Orange Pudding]

Queso
[Cheese]

Galletas
[Crackers]

Cafe Negro
[Black Coffee]

DINNER, 75 Cents

Cabaret Dancers
Casa Verdugo Cafe, Los Angeles

"ENSALADAS ESPANOL" (SPANISH SALADS)

Prepared Vinegar for Spanish Salad Dressing

Put a button of garlic, large slice cucumber, slice onion, tablespoon parsley, tablespoon taragon leaves, or two tablespoons taragon vinegar into one pint cider vinegar. Bottle and let stand several days, strain and keep for following salads and dressings.

Especially Prepared Dressings

Spanish Dressing No. 1

Rub mixing bowl with button of garlic, break into bowl one egg yolk, whip stiff, add one-fourth cup best olive oil slowly, then one-fourth cup lemon juice, tablespoon prepared vinegar, teaspoon sugar, half teaspoon salt, tablespoon green chile pulp. Very fine.

Spanish Dressing No. 2

Six tablespoons of best olive oil in bowl, add gradually three tablespoons lemon juice and one of prepared vinegar, one teaspoon brown sugar, half teaspoon salt, tablespoon red chile pulp, stir with rotary motion until a thick cream, serve at once on salad.

Spanish Salad Dressing No. 3

Lemon or lime juice. Six tablespoons to three of olive oil, teaspoon sugar, one-half teaspoon salt, dash red pepper, teaspoon onion juice.

Spanish Salad, Avacado (Aligator Pear)

Peel and cut in half pears, sprinkle with salt and sugar twenty minutes before using, then place in heart of small crisp lettuce head, pour over Spanish dressing No. 3.

Tomato and Cucumber Salad

Select six fine ripe tomatoes; remove the hearts carefully; place on ice until chilled; pare two cucumbers and chop them finely; mix with tomato pulp; pour over a half cup of dressing No. 3 and fill the tomatoes. Serve on lettuce leaves and decorate with thinly sliced sweet peppers.

Spanish Sweet Pepper Salad

Remove seed and fill half peppers with chopped cucumber and celery, mixed with dressing No. 3, garnish with pimiento or beets, serve on lettuce.

Spanish Bean Salad

One cup Spanish beans cooked tender, small pink (canned red kidney beans will do); chop sweet green pepper, one-fourth cup, tablespoon each of onion, ripe sweet pepper, parsley and cucumber, mix with beans, serve with Spanish dressing No. 1.

Spanish Tomato and Egg Salad

Peel smooth just ripe tomatoes, slice in three slices across, place on lettuce leaf, put border around of hard boiled whites of eggs, stand hard boiled yolk in center, pour over Spanish dressing No. 1.

Stuffed Tomato Salad

Scald and peel large tomatoes, remove center, mix with equal parts celery, green chile, onions, fry in little olive oil and lemon juice, salt to taste, fill tomatoes, teaspoon Spanish dressing No. 1, sprinkle little chopped parsley and grated cheese, set on ice, serve on lettuce.

Spanish California Ripe Olive Salad

Remove seed from ripe olives, fill with mixture of cottage cheese, pimiento, salt, paprika, parsley, press together, serve on lettuce leaf, cover with Spanish dressing No. 1.

Spanish Moulded Salad

Chop enough ripe tomatoes to fill a cup, half cup cucumber, one-fourth cup celery, one-fourth cup green sweet peppers, tablespoon onion, one-half teaspoon chile powder, salt to taste. Dissolve one tablespoon gelatine in one cup tomato juice, pour over above, mix and mould, when firm cut in squares, serve with Spanish sauce Nos. 1 or 2 in lettuce leaf.

Spanish Cucumber and Tomato Salad

Pare and chop fine one good-sized fresh cucumber. Shred sufficient cabbage to make one pint, throw in cold water for one hour; scald and peel one good sized tomato and chop fine. Remove the seeds from one large sweet pepper, chop and mix with the tomato. When ready to serve drain and dry the cabbage. Put into salad bowl a layer of cabbage, then a layer of cucumber, then a layer of tomato and a layer of pepper; sprinkle with a few drops of onion juice; then another layer of cabbage and continue until all the material is used. Serve with dressing No. 2.

Spanish Cabbage Salad

Two cups shredded cabbage red and white mixed, two tablespoons chopped roasted chestnuts, two of pecans, mix with dressing No. 2 and serve in lettuce cups.

Rice Salad

A cup of boiled rice; four hard-boiled eggs, and one head of lettuce. Arrange on platter, alternate layers of rice, shredded lettuce leaves, slices of hard-boiled eggs and dressing No. 1. Over the top layer of dressing press the yolk of an egg through a sieve and garnish the edges with a layer of lettuce leaves and radish tulip. Chop cress and cabbage, equal parts, add few minced chives, add one-fourth cup cream to one-half cup salad dressing No. 3 and serve over salad.

Oven in Patio, Ramona's Marriage Place

Old Spanish Kitchen in California

Indian Ovens

SOPA ESPANOL
(SPANISH SOUPS)

Sopa de Frijoles (Bean Soup)

Cook one pint pink beans in two quarts beef stock till tender. Add one cup chopped onions, two green, two ripe chiles (fresh or canned), one quart canned tomatoes, two tablespoons chopped parsley. Cook all thoroughly. Drop in Spanish meat balls and serve with Spanish cheese fingers.

Spanish Meat Balls

Grind soup beef very fine. Add one egg to one cup meat, salt, little onion juice, two tablespoons soaked bread, make into very small balls, roll in crumbs, fry, drop in soup just before serving and sprinkle each ball with finely chopped parsley and bits of pimiento for color effect.

Sopa de Papas (Potato Soup)

Add one cup mashed potatoes to one cup chicken, veal or beef stock, one cup milk, tablespoon butter, salt, one bay leaf, tablespoon flour to thicken, cook and strain, cut thinly sliced bread, round, the size of a nickle, butter and toast, make little pile grated yellow cheese on toast, top with red sweet pepper, pinch of chopped parsley on top. Serve hot.

Spanish Hot Vegetable Broth

Make broth of one cup cabbage, one cup carrots, one-half cup onions, one cup garlic, one-half cup turnips, one-half cup celery, one-fourth cup green pepper. Add one quart canned tomatoes, one quart clarified meat stock, cook thoroughly, strain, serve hot with spoonful well cooked rice in bowl. For vegetable soup leave all vegetables in.

Spanish Fish Chowder

Fry one-half cup salt pork cut into small cubes, one-half cup chopped onion to light brown, add tablespoon flour, then add two cups small pieces of white boneless fish meat, brown slightly, strain two cups hot milk, one cup prepared Spanish sauce, salt to taste, dash of paprika. Clams or oysters may be used, allowing only one minute for clams or oysters.

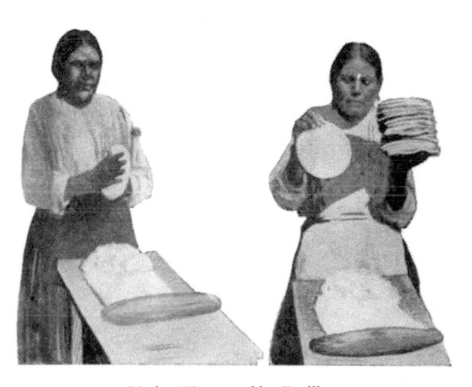

Mexican Woman making Tortillas

Y. Y. Perez, Public Bakery, Sonora Town, Los Angeles. They refuse to make them any other way and take the same pleasure in making a perfectly thin and round tortilla that puffs up nicely while cooking, as you and I do in trying to make a beautiful loaf of bread. Truly the heart of women are the same the world over. Deep down, no matter what the environment, the desire is always there, to be "loaf givers."

TORTILLAS

Modern Way to Prepare Corn for Tortilla and Tamales

Put one gallon of shelled corn in enough water to cover; dissolve one-half cup lime in a little water and add to cover; boil fifteen or twenty minutes; remove from fire, pour off first water and add fresh cold water; rub with hand to remove husk. Rinse in another water and it is ready to grind. Don't wash too much or it will not be pasty enough to make tortilla.

Tortillas No. 2

Another way and liked best by some people: Add to the corn dough (masa) rounding tablespoon of lard to four cups dough, little salt.

Tortillas No. 3

Still another way: Corn meal and coarse flour half and half wet to stiff dough, salt and lard.

Tortillas No. 4

But the best to my taste is the hominy or corn ground into a smooth paste, three cups corn, one of flour, two tablespoons melted lard, teaspoon salt, cook on ungreased iron, have ready enough hot salted lard to dip tortilla in just before you add filling to make Enchiladas. When flour is used, dough may be rolled out on a board, a small pie tin placed on and cut round the edge to form cake; lift up with pancake turner.

How to Shape Tortillas

Take piece of dough size of biscuit and press with hand into cake size of small pie plate, toast on top of stove moderately warm. Do not brown.

A Plate of Tortilla

Taco

Made by putting chopped cooked beef and chile sauce in tortilla made of meal and flour; folded, edges sealed together with egg; fried in deep fat, chile sauce served over it.

Indian Woman baking Bread

A Public Bakery in Mexico
Women making Tortilla

Enchiladas

ENCHILADAS

Enchiladas, No. 1 (Very fine)

Make Tortilla. Chop one cup onions very fine, slice and chop one-half cup olives, cook in little lard; have cup grated cheese ready, dip tortilla in hot salted lard, dip in chile sauce No. 1, spread with grated cheese, put in center tablespoonful of cooked onions, tablespoon chopped hard-boiled eggs, two tablespoons chopped chicken, six seedless raisins soaked in claret, level tablespoon chopped olives, a sprinkle of cheese and fourth cup Chile Sauce No. 1, fold both sides, one over the other, pour Chile Sauce No. 5 over all, put tablespoon cooked onion on center of top of each and several large pieces of cheese and three whole olives. Place in hot oven till cheese is melted, serve very hot.

Enchiladas No. 2

Use green chile sauce for Enchiladas No. 2, and filling of beef or veal, with onion or coddled or poached egg on top sprinkled with grated cheese, spoonful red chile sauce dropped in spots for color, heat till cheese melts.

CHILE PULP AND SAUCES FOR ALL RECIPES

Chile peppers are the base of all Mexican and Spanish dishes, and I have simplified the various recipes by making a list of different ways to make the pepper pulps and sauces. Please note that they are numbered and named, referred to by number and name in the recipes. Original way to prepare chile for sauce is to remove seed and toast on coals, top of stove or in oven, till they puff and look tender; and mash through sieve or colander; add water or tomatoes for right consistency; scalding is the quickest.

No. 1, Red Chile Sauce, for Enchiladas or Tamales, etc.

Split red chile pepper, remove all seeds and veins, soak several hours in water, pour off, pour on boiling water, pour off and repeat again, the last water just enough to cover peppers when pressed down. Mash in this water and press through sieve, melt one-half cup pure lard, add heaping tablespoon flour, brown and add three cups of chile pulp, salt to taste, cook very slowly half hour.

No. 2, Green Chile Sauce for Enchiladas or Tamales, etc.

Split, remove seeds and veins from green chiles and boil in little hot water till tender; mash, press through sieve, melt one-fourth cup lard, add two tablespoons flour, teaspoon salt, brown just a little, add three cups green pulp, cook slowly half hour.

Prepared Spanish Sauce

Take equal parts red and green chile peppers, same amount green and red sweet peppers, split, remove seed from all, soak in water, drain, add enough water to barely cover, boil tender, mash in water, press through sieve, heat half cup olive oil, fry in it one-half cup onion, one-half parsley, three garlic buttons, tablespoon aregano, two cups raw tomatoes, six cloves, two cups of the pepper pulp, salt to taste, cook, strain, may heat and bottle larger quantities, very fine.

PICKLES AND RELISHES

Spanish Pickle

Heat quart apple vinegar, add tablespoon salt, twenty cloves, two tablespoons aregano, two of cominos, boil five minutes, let cool, pour over small red and green chiles, wild tamatillos (wild tomatoes) and put up in jars.

Green Chile Relish, No. 1

Remove seed and veins from twelve large green chiles, soak over night in water with little salt in it, chop and measure one quart green tomatoes, chop chiles, one cup cucumber, 1 garlic button, cook altogether until a pulp, press through sieve, add one-half cup lemon or lime juice, tablespoon salt. Fine over cold meats, fish, oysters, eggs, croquettes, roast pork, mix with apple sauce; serve on fried apple fritters.

Red Chile Relish, No. 2

Make same as green, substitute ripe tomatoes and red chiles. You may bottle, seal tightly each sauce; will keep indefinitely.

CHILE CON CARNE

Mexican Red Hot Chile Con Carne

To each cup of raw or cooked, chopped or ground beef, one-half cup lard or suet, add one cup pulp of red chile pepper, two cups beef stock, salt, cook until a thick sauce is formed, serve with frijoles.

Chicken Giblet Chile

Cook chicken jiblets livers and hearts tender in small amount water; chop and add equal amount chile sauce No. 1 or 2, salt to taste, serve on Spanish rice put in dish, sprinkle with parmasan cheese or Mexican grated cheese.

Chile Con Carne (Mild)

Two cups cooked chopped beef, one-half cup green chile pulp, one-half cup suet, tablespoon lard, one cup tomatoes, one button garlic, one-half cup chopped onion. Cook until thick, serve with frijoles.

Chile Con Carne

One-half cup chopped salt pork, one-half cup suet, add one-half cup chopped onion, one teaspoon aregano, one-half teaspoon safron, fry all together; add two cups cooked ground beef, two cups frijoles, two cups red chile pulp, one cup water or three cups water and four tablespoons chile powder, salt to taste and cook forty minutes.

Chicken Chile

Boil a fat chicken in small amount water with garlic button, or slice of onion to flavor. When tender chop the meat in small pieces, heat some of the chicken fat skimmed from the liquor and cut from chicken, add flour, bit of onion, add one cup green chile pulp, two cups of water chicken was boiled in, salt; add chopped chicken, stew few minutes, serve on Spanish rice.

Chile Con Carne

Cook beef, veal or chicken with parsley, carrots, celery, onions, bay leaf. Let it cook very slowly until tender, then cut meat into small pieces, strain the juice, add to every pint one-half cup chile pulp and one cup of cooked and mashed frijoles, add tablespoon butter or lard, then meat, and if too hot add cup tomatoes, cook few minutes longer.

Tamales

Chop one pound of beef, pork or chicken, add a little chopped tallow or one tablespoonful of lard and a little salt; fry in a pan until tender; chop again very fine; return to pan; add a little warm water and pulp of two red chiles; stir and fry few minutes. Add to one quart of cornmeal two tablespoonfuls of salt, two table-spoonfuls of lard, and boiling water to make a thick dough. Cut off about one inch of corn husk stalk ends and soak in hot water ten minutes; dry and rub over with hot lard. Put a layer of dough on the husk about four inches long, one and one-half inches wide and one-fourth inch thick; along the center spread two teaspoonfuls of the prepared meat; roll and fold the small end of the husk; place them folded end down in a strainer over hot water. Cover and steam several hours. Serve hot.

TAMALES

Chicken Tamales

Soak some trimmed corn husk (bought in Mexican stores) for several hours in cold water, then boil until soft, remove; dry on cloth, and rub with lard. Cut up a fat chicken, cook until very tender in just enough water to leave about four cups. Chop up cooked chicken, add corn meal or masa to boiling hot chicken broth until a thick dough; add salt to taste, one tablespoon chile powder, or chile sauce No. 1; add tablespoon of lard and knead all together until light and smooth. Now to all the chicken add enough chile sauce No. 1 to mix thickly together; add about one-fourth cup of sliced olives and a few whole ones and one-fourth cup seedless raisins, and a few whole ones, salt to taste and cook together for five minutes; spread corn dough evenly over shuck or husk about one-eighth inch thick. In center of one larger husk place a large kitchen spoonful of chicken; spread over this one tablespoonful of dough; place another husk spread with dough; continue placing husk around on all sides until about ten are used. Tie ends together with a strip of husk and place on end in a colander over boiling water for two or three hours, or place some corn husk in bottom of vessel, pile tamales on top, pour in about a quart of water, bring to a boil and steam slowly for three or four hours.

Tamale Pie

Make a crust of two cups of hot water, one-half cup lard, one teaspoon salt, and cornmeal to make thick dough. Spread on bottom and sides of pie tin. Mix beef, pork, veal or chicken with plenty of suet for shortening—any two of above meats will do—measure two cups of meat, add two tablespoons of cornmeal, one-half cup of chile pulp, one teaspoon salt, one-half cup meat stock or water. Cook for a few minutes, fill pie crust, spread more dough over top. Make little balls the size of marbles set around edge. Pour a little melted lard over the top, sprinkle with chile powder; bake about thirty minutes.

Beef Tamales

Ground beef fried in lard and suet, add chile sauce No. 2 and cook until thick. Prepare cornmeal or masa by pouring on boiling hot water, salt to taste, add one cup of lard to four cups meal or masa, add few olives and raisins if desired. Prepare as for chicken tamale recipe. Steam. Texas tamales made as above with olives and raisins left out and spoonful put in one long shuck, fold ends over and press flat.

Corn Husk and Red Chile

There are firms in California putting up a specially prepared corn meal for tortillas. There are chile powders and canned red and green hot chile peppers; also the red sweet pepper, called pimiento, which makes it possible to cook Spanish dishes anywhere.

EGGS ESPANOL
(EGGS COOKED SPANISH)

Spanish Omelet (Supreme)

A complete lesson—Fry a strip of bacon for each diner; remove from fat and keep hot. Cook until tender, in the fat, one tablespoon minced onion and sliver of garlic button (young green onion is best), one tablespoon minced green sweet pepper, same of canned sweet red pepper (pimiento), one tablespoon parsley, four sliced ripe olives, four seedless raisins, six mushrooms. Add when done, level teaspoon flour, then add one cup tomato—raw or canned; cook few minutes, salt to taste, add one teaspoon chile powder or two tablespoons red chile sauce. Use the above amount for every two eggs. Keep hot and prepare eggs by breaking in separate bowl whites and yolk; beat yolk first very stiff till light in color, add tablespoon water to each yolk and one-eighth teaspoon salt. Beat whites stiff, add small pinch cream tartar while whipping. Fold three-fourths of the whites into the yolks—do not break up too fine. Have hot omelet pan bottom covered well with lard or butter; pour in eggs; lower fire and cook slowly, lifting up with spatula at different places to let raw egg to bottom. When nearly done, set under gas broiler or in very hot oven for a few minutes until seared. Remove, and with spoon, put prepared filling on one-half of omelet, fold other half over, turn out on a hot platter. Put rest of whipped whites on top to form a circular crown around edge. Sprinkle with salt and bits of butter; set back in oven and brown but not too deeply. Remove; decorate with bits or strips of pimiento, sliced olives, parsley, and last, the strips of bacon and triangles of toast. A simple way, not so pretty and fluffy, but good, is to mix the filling with whipped eggs; cook, fold and serve hot.

Spanish Stuffed Tomato Omelet

Soak one cup bread crumbs in one-half cup boiling milk, add tablespoon butter, salt, pepper, teaspoon onion juice. Remove centers from peeled tomatoes, stuff with bread mixture, place in a serving platter, bake until tender. Whip one egg for each tomato separately. Add tablespoon water to each yolk, salt, chile pepper, teaspoon butter for each egg. Pour around tomatoes to come to top. Bake in moderate oven. Serve hot, or partly fill tomato with bread mixture, break egg on top, sprinkle with cheese and bake. Cut tomatoes out in squares to get all the egg, and serve on lettuce.

Eggs in Chile Blankets

Roll a long piece of cheese in strips of chile peppers roasted, peeled and seeded, fry in hot lard and serve with prepared Spanish sauce on toast.

Spanish Sausage Omelet

Mix level tablespoon fine sausage, tablespoon bread crumbs in tablespoon milk for each egg, whip yolks of as many eggs as needed, little parsley, salt and teaspoon red pepper pulp, or chile powder; add white of egg and pour into hot greased pan; cook slowly, until done. Fold and turn out, cover with Spanish sauce. Garnish with lettuce or parsley.

Spanish Creamed Eggs

Boil eggs hard fifteen minutes, shell, cut lengthwise; remove yolk (reserve one egg). Mash yolk and add to each a teaspoon of thick white sauce, or bread cooked smooth in milk; bits of butter, pinch of salt, paprika and finely minced parsley. Fill white of eggs, fasten together with toothpicks; roll in raw egg and bread crumbs; fry in deep hot olive oil or other fat; drain. Remove toothpicks and where eggs are put together separate with knife and sprinkle center with little crumbled dry yolk, place on toast. Make a border of chopped whites cut in rings. Pour hot Spanish sauce partly over and around egg; garnish with parsley, and you have a delicious dish in truly Spanish colors.

Mexican Scrambled Eggs in Chile

Mix one tablespoon green chile pulp to each egg, whipped separately, teaspoon lard or butter, a slice garlic or teaspoon onion juice, scramble quickly, serve on toast, garnish with spoonful red chile sauce and parsley.

Pimiento Egg

Hard boil small eggs, shell, salt, put each in a canned pimiento large enough to close end with toothpick, salt well, dip in batter, fry in deep fat, slice in half lengthwise, make cup white sauce, add tablespoon green chile pulp, serve on egg, good and pretty Spanish color effect.

Spanish Eggs in Peppers

Scald large sweet peppers; peel, cut in half, remove seeds, half fill with minced onion fried brown, one teaspoon red chile sauce, tablespoon tomato sauce or catsup. Break one egg and scramble and pile on top. Decorate with red chile powder and parsley. Or break egg whole on top of sauce and bake in oven.

Spanish Eggs, Shirred

Brown in a teaspoon of butter or bacon fat, one teaspoon of minced onion, add teaspoon of flour, salt to taste, one teaspoon prepared chile sauce, one-fourth cup raw tomato. Cook and pour into individual baking dish and break egg over top. Set in oven until eggs are covered with a film. Garnish with sprigs of parsley and serve hot.

"CARNE ESPANOL"
(SPANISH MEATS)

Spanish Steak (Elegante)

Slightly grease very hot skillet with olive oil. Select tender steak, sear both sides, turning until cooked as desired. Make ready a sauce as follows: Melt two tablespoons butter, one of olive oil together, add tablespoon onion, one small button of garlic, one tablespoon parsley, one green sweet pepper, and two tablespoons chili pulp. When well browned, add tablespoon flour and brown, add one can prepared tomato soup or two cups fresh chopped tomatoes, cook five minutes, strain and pour over hot steak. Garnish with mushrooms and ripe olives browned in butter, sprinkled with salt and chile pepper and sprigs of parsley, or if cheese is liked, sprinkle grated yellow cheese over steak and sauce, melt in oven, serve hot, or use Spanish prepared sauce.

Spanish Steak (Economical)

Select two pounds upper round steak, sear on hot skillet on both sides till crust is formed; then one-half cup suet, half cup hot water, cover; cook slowly half hour, add salt and pepper. Fry one cup chopped onions in tablespoon lard until slightly brown; add tablespoon flour, can tomatoes, teaspoon oregano, two tablespoons green chile pulp; spread over steak, cover and cook twenty minutes longer. Place on serving dish, sprinkle with cheese, set in oven to melt cheese and serve hot.

Flank Steak, Spanish

Have butcher cris cross a flank steak. Rub into it flour, seasoned with salt and chile powder, not too much, spread with lard or melted suet, make a filling of bread crumbs, tomato, chile pulp or powder, onion, aregano, bay leaf, salt, roll up and tie. Put tablespoon lard, cup tomato, little salt on top, cover and bake two or three hours slowly.

Spanish Pork Tenderloin Cutlets

Pound tenderloin out flat; cover with flour, seasoned with salt, pepper and chili powder. Fry brown in hot olive oil or bacon fat. Place triangles of toast in center of platter, arrange cutlets standing around toast. Put lettuce cups around outside of cutlets and fill with half of peeled tomato, sprinkled with cooked rice and parsley, salt and chile powder, or, tomatoes stuffed with a mixture of meat and rice, seasoned with salt, chile powder, onion and butter. Bake until brown on top. Garnish with parsley and set twig of parsley in center of toast.

Mexican Meat Cakes

Mix pork sausage and hamburger equal parts, to two cups meat add one cup wet bread, add one egg, one-fourth cup onion, teaspoon salt, tablespoon green chile pulp, mix and make into cakes one inch thick, put one cup prepared sauce in pan and heat, place meat in sauce, cover, simmer till done.

Spanish Meat Cakes (Delicious)

Use finely ground beef, veal or chicken—raw or cooked. To each cup meat, add one-half cup wet bread crumbs, one-fourth cup chopped mushrooms, browned in a little butter, teaspoon onion juice, one-fourth cup white sauce and salt to taste. Make into round flat cakes; fry in small amount olive oil and butter, until brown; make a sauce of six chopped olives, one-fourth cup mushrooms, tablespoon onion, tablespoon flour in tablespoon each of olive oil and butter; add salt and paprika, and cup of fresh or canned tomatoes, and tablespoon green chile pulp, and pour around meat cakes. Sprinkle with chopped parsley.

Mexican Meat Dumplings

Mix one cup meat raw or cooked, add one-half cup chopped bacon, one-half cup tomatoes, teaspoon salt, tablespoon chile pulp or chile powder, mix to thick dough with corn meal, make into balls size of walnuts, drop in salted boiling water and tomatoes, little lard and corn meal to thicken water when meat is done.

Spanish Beef Stew

Cut one pound stew beef or veal in small two-inch pieces, flour thickly and brown in tablespoon of hot suet; add one-half cup chopped onion, one bay leaf, four cups tomatoes; cook slowly until meat is tender; add salt, one tablespoon chile pulp; one cup cold boiled potatoes—cut in neat squares. When potatoes are hot, serve on triangles of buttered toast.

Mexican Chicken Meat Balls

Two cups ground chicken, two tablespoons finely chopped onion, one-half cup tomato, one-half garlic button, two tablespoons chopped sweet pepper, one egg, one teaspoon mint leaves, one-half teaspoon aregano, one teaspoon salt, one tablespoon butter, three tablespoons corn meal mush, mix together, roll in flour, make into balls, fry in deep fat, or bake in oven, serve with Spanish sauce.

Spanish Fish Stew

Cut fish in three-inch pieces, salt and roll in corn meal. Heat tablespoon bacon fat and one of olive oil, add half cup sliced onion, fry brown, add fish and brown, add enough tomato to barely cover fish, two tablespoons chile sauce, salt to taste, pinch safron, and aregano; cook few minutes. Serve on platter. Garnish with potato balls sprinkled with chopped parsley.

Spanish Baked Fish

Make a filling of bread crumbs wet with one cup of tomatoes, add one tablespoon minced onion, one tablespoon parsley, one-half cup red tomato pulp, two tablespoons melted butter, ten sliced olives, one-half cup seedless raisins; fill and sew up fish. Place in pan. When done, remove carefully to hot platter and peel off skin. Pour hot prepared Spanish sauce over fish; garnish with lemon and parsley. Awfully good.

Spanish Fried Fish

Salt and dip Barracuda or any tender fish in a batter made of egg, flour, milk and salt. Fry in deep hot olive oil. Serve with sauce made by browning tablespoon onion in tablespoon olive oil, adding tablespoon flour and browning, then add one cup tomatoes, two tablespoons green or red chile pulp, salt; cook and pour across center of fish, allowing brown crisp ends to show. Garnish with slices of sweet green pepper, lemon and parsley.

Spanish Hash

Put a layer of seasoned whipped potatoes one inch thick in a shallow baking pan. Another layer of finely chopped beef, lamb, veal, fish, or fowl; seasoned with salt and pepper and a little onion browned in lard; prepare a top layer of one cup onions, one green and one sweet red pepper, one tablespoon parsley, teaspoon chili powder or pulp, salt, tablespoon flour—all browned in two tablespoons lard. Add one-half can tomatoes; cook till thick; spread over meat layer, sprinkle with bread crumbs, bits of cheese and bake. Dainty when baked in individual dishes.

Spanish Curry Hash

Brown in two tablespoons butter, three tablespoons chopped onions, one cup ground meat,—one or more kinds, one cup tomatoes, ten sliced olives, one tablespoon Worcestershire sauce, one chopped green sweet pepper, one-fourth teaspoon curry powder, one tablespoon flour; add cup of any meat stock or hot water; salt to taste; add one cup cooked rice; alternate in layer with hash. Pour little butter over top and bake. Garnish with parsley and slices of hard cooked egg.

Spanish Stewed Rabbit

Gut and roll rabbit in meal and flour, salt and chile powder, fry nice brown, cover with Spanish sauce, little hot water, add one-half cup raisins, stew ten minutes, garnish with toast and mint.

Spanish Chicken Stew

Cut up tender chicken, salt and flour, brown in small amount of olive oil. Keep hot. Add tablespoon butter to oil left in frying pan; add one-half cup onions, one small clove of garlic, tablespoon parsley, two tablespoons flour; brown all together and add two cups tomatoes, two tablespoons chile pulp and one teaspoon sugar; cook until thick; pour over chicken; garnish with buttered toast and green peas.

Spanish Style Stuffed Chicken

Brown a fat tender chicken in a small amount of lard by turning over and over for a few minutes. Make a dressing of two cups bread crumbs, three tablespoons pulp of sweet green peppers, one cup tomatoes, two tablespoons chopped onion, one-half cup claret, two tablespoons sugar, one-half cup sliced onions, one-half cup seeded raisins, one teaspoon white pepper, and salt to taste. Stuff chicken and bake in closed pan one hour. Make gravy of drippings by adding flour, mushroom sauce and hot water. Pour over chicken.

Spanish Baked Chicken En Casserole

Salt a tender chicken, rub inside and out with onion, butter and flour. Put in a large casserole. Pour in bottom one cup hot water, one teaspoon oregano; add can mushrooms, stems and trimmings; one dozen sliced olives, two tablespoons green Spanish sauce, and one chopped pimiento, two cups of tomatoes, one tablespoon butter and tablespoon flour to thicken; salt to taste; cover and cook till done; add cup of cream and cook ten to fifteen minutes longer. Dip buttered toast in sherry— enough toast for each guest; lay on top of chicken; cover; let stand few minutes. Serve from casserole.

Spanish Dressing for Chicken or Turkey

One pint of cold corn bread, one cup rich chicken or turkey broth, one-half cup roasted chopped chestnuts, one tablespoon butter, one hard-boiled egg minced, one teaspoon black pepper, three tablespoons red chile pulp, one-fourth cup minced onion, large tablespoon minced parsley, one egg whipped very light, salt to taste, stuff turkey or chicken, when baked, make the ordinary dressing of the drippings and chile sauce, to serve on dressing.

Spanish Tripe

In three tablespoons butter, fry one-half cup onion. Cut one pound tripe into narrow strips; salt and roll in flour. Add one tablespoon flour to fat and brown; add to this one cup tomato, season with tablespoon chile powder or pulp, one teaspoon sugar. Let simmer until very tender. Serve hot.

FRIJOLES
(SPANISH BEANS)

How to Cook Beans

Soak over night, put in fresh water in the morning and add one-fourth teaspoon of soda to each quart of water, boil until half done, drain and add more boiling water and cook till tender. Boil longer when they are to be mashed.

Frijoles (Bean) Sauce

Cook red Spanish beans tender, put in pan with hot lard, add onions, green or red chile pulp, salt, brown a little flour with it, mash, press through sieve, add meat stock to thin for sauce, serve over meat or whole beans.

Frijoles

Soak pink or kidney beans over night, boil till tender in salted water with pinch soda. Drain and add can tomatoes, pulp of three red and three green chile peppers, one-half cup onions fried in bacon fat, salt to taste, boil slowly till very soft.

Spanish Mashed Baked Beans

Cook pink or kidney beans in salted water with pinch of soda until very soft. Drain and mash, fry bacon crisp, remove from pan and turn beans into fat, let brown and turn out on hot platter, pour hot Spanish sauce over, garnish with bacon and parsley.

Spanish Beans Au Gratin

Two cups of well-cooked beans, drained of water—into two tablespoons of hot lard, two tablespoons of red chile pulp; brown; add one-half cup grated cheese, stir until melted. Serve piping hot.

ARROZ A LA ESPANOL
(SPANISH RICE)

How to Cook Rice

Wash rice in several waters, drain, rub between towels until dry, throw the rice spoonful at a time, one cup to five cups, into boiling hot salted water, boil hard for ten minutes then slowly until all water is absorbed, put asbestos mat under vessel and do not stir; grains will be dry and separate from each other.

Spanish Rice—Mint Flavor

Heat two tablespoons lard, bacon or olive oil, add tablespoon chopped onion, one-half teaspoon salt, one-half teaspoon chile powder, pinch of mint leaves, slightly cook, add one cup rice and stir about until rice begins to color, add four cups hot water, cook slowly until all water is absorbed. Pile on platter and cover with Spanish sauce.

Spanish Rice

Fry heaping tablespoon chipped bacon, add one garlic, stir, cook few minutes, add one cup washed and dried rice, one can tomatoes, salt, add one-half cup chile pulp, cook slowly; when about dry, add meat stock or hot water to finish cooking, but just enough to have rice dry and grains separated when done.

Spanish Rice au Gratin

Boil one cup rice in five cups water, add a button of garlic, teaspoon salt; when done remove garlic. Drain any water and put in baking vessel alternate layers of rice, Spanish sauce and cheese, topping with sauce and cheese on top. Bake until hot through and cheese a rich brown.

Green Peppers With Rice

Chop two tablespoons onion, two tablespoons red sweet peppers, two tablespoons green sweet peppers very fine, fry until tender with a tablespoon chopped salt pork. Add two cups tomatoes, cook and add tablespoon chile pepper, salt, fill green sweet peppers, put butter on top, sprinkle of brown sugar, lemon juice; bake.

SPANISH STUFFED PEPPERS AND ONIONS

Stuffed Chile Pepper

Fry chile peppers until they puff under skin; cool and peel; cut out stem, and with a spoon remove seed. Prepare a mixture of any kind of meat, to a cup of meat, one tablespoon of chopped onion, one clove garlic, one-half cup tomatoes, one-half cup of sliced olives, one-fourth raisins—chopped very fine. Add one tablespoon vinegar, and cook in two tablespoons hot lard; cool and fill the chile peppers. Beat desired number of eggs separately, add a tablespoon flour, one of milk to each egg, and season with salt and red pepper. Dip chile in batter, and fry brown in hot lard, drain, sprinkle with chopped parsley; serve hot. A prepared sauce may be served over chile or a white sauce with apple, raisins, peach preserves or marmalades added to desired taste. Delicious.

Spanish Stuffed Sweet Peppers

Mix one cup of ground meat, any kind, with half cup bread, two tablespoons onion, one-half cup tomatoes, one tablespoon sugar, one-half raisins, cook all together in one tablespoon hot butter for a few minutes, cool, add one egg, salt, chile powder, fill large sweet pepper that has all seed removed, set close together and fill in between with raw tomato, salt, pinch aregano to reach top of tomatoes, sprinkle with bread crumbs and bake until well done and brown.

Sweet Spanish Peppers With Sardines

Roast or scald and peel green sweet peppers, take out seed and veins, mix with half cup vinegar, half cup water, add one-half garlic button, one-half teaspoon aregano, piece of cinnamon; soak all night. Make filling of one-half cup bread, tablespoon onion, one-half cup tomatoes, tablespoon sliced olives, six seedless raisins, drain peppers and fill. Cover with melted butter, bread and grated cheese. Bake and serve hot.

Spanish Cheese and Pepper Fritters

Heat and peel green hot or sweet peppers; remove seed and fill with salt and red pepper, mixture of cheese and bread, wet in tomato juice—half and half—fasten with toothpicks; dip in egg and roll in bread; fry in deep fat; serve with Spanish sauce and circle of hard-boiled eggs.

Chiles Stuffed With Cheese

Mix half cup bread wet with one-half cup tomatoes and one-half cup Queso Mexicano (a Mexican cheese), tablespoon onion, one-half button garlic, tablespoon parsley, salt, pepper, one-fourth cup sliced olives, mushroom or raisins chopped and fried in tablespoon lard until tender. Add the bread and cheese, when cool, stuff chiles, dip in the egg batter and fry in deep fat or saute in butter. To be eaten hot served with or without sauce.

Spanish Onion

Grind one cup raw liver to a pulp, remove strings, add one whipped egg, one tablespoon onion juice, one-fourth cup cracker crumbs wet, one and one-half cup milk, one-half teaspoon salt; fill boiled onions (centers removed); cover with grated cheese, cover and cook until liver is firm. Remove cover, brown slightly, serve with a prepared Spanish sauce.

Spanish Onions

Brown two tablespoons of flour in two tablespoons butter; add two tablespoons chopped onion, two tablespoons sliced olives, two tablespoons raisins, chopped sour pickle, one tablespoon parsley, two tablespoons chopped nuts, one-half cup bread crumbs, one-half cup cooked chicken, pork or veal, one teaspoon salt. Fill onions that have been boiled tender, and centers removed—pile high—put large lump cheese on top and bake. Serve with sauce made of one tablespoon butter, one tablespoon flour, two tablespoons lemon juice, one-half cup water and finely chopped parsley.

Spanish Stuffed Potatoes

Rub lard on large smooth potatoes. Bake until soft; cut off a slice and cut out center of potatoes, add two tablespoons butter, one tablespoon of finely cut parsley, two tablespoons of pimiento—chopped—cucumber, chopped—one-fourth teaspoon chile powder, two tablespoons hot milk, one-half whipped egg; beat up until light, fill potato shell. Place two strips of bacon on top, set in oven until bacon is crisp. Garnish with stripe of pimiento and parsley.

Mexican Baked Macaroni or Spaghetti

Cook and drain macaroni or spaghetti, two cups of either; heat one-fourth cup olive oil, add clove of garlic and one-half cup chipped dried beef, cook until beef curls, add tablespoon flour, brown, add one-half cup chopped mushrooms, two tablespoons green chile pulp, one large pimiento chopped fine, add two cups tomatoes, cook all together, salt to taste, mix with macaroni, put in baking dish, cover with grated Mexican cheese (Queso Mexicano), bake till cheese is melted.

Calabasas (Summer Squash)

Cook round summer squash in salted water until tender; remove centers. Mix with egg, bread crumbs and grated cheese, salt and chile powder. Fill center of squash, pile high, sprinkle with cheese, and bits of butter; bake in a hot oven. Garnish with bits of red chile pepper and chopped parsley mixed with a little hot butter.

FINIS

Spanish Cheese Fingers

To serve with all salads. Make very short pie paste with butter, salt; roll and fold several times, sprinkle with grated cheese and chile pepper; roll it into paste enough to make it stick, cut in strips, bake in hot oven, tie in bunches with red ribbon, garnish with sprig of parsley, or cut strips of bread; cover with paste of melted cheese and chile pepper, toast in oven, serve with salads.

Mexican Sandwiches

Remove seeds from chiles, green and red, if canned, chop fine; if raw, roast or scald and peel; first fry separately in a little butter, salt to taste, little lemon juice, don't brown. Spread between layers of thickly cut white and brown bread alternately, with one slice of bread buttered and sprinkle thickly with grated cheese; the color effect is pretty when cut in fancy shapes and served on crisp lettuce leaf, or mix red and green chile together; fry, cool, add grated cheese, spread on tortillas that have been dipped in hot butter, roll lightly, fasten with toothpick; garnish with sprig parsley; serve on crisp lettuce leaves.

Spanish Brown Cake

Cream two cups brown sugar with one cup butter, pour around this one cup sweet or sour milk, whip four eggs and pour on top, add three cups flour with three teaspoons baking powder sifted through, two teaspoons cinnamon, mix and pour into baking tins, sprinkle top with brown sugar, ground pecans and cinnamon while raw; bake in medium oven. Or add enough flour on rolling board to make a soft dough, cut into large round buns; bake and spread with icing made of hot water and brown sugar cooked until thick with pecan nuts added.

Spanish Chocolate Cake

Get the Spanish chocolate, a little round cake about three inches across, flavor different from other chocolate. Melt two cakes, add one-half cup butter, one cup brown sugar, beat four eggs separately, mix yolk into chocolate, butter and sugar, beat well, pour one cup milk on top, the beaten egg white on top of milk, three cups flour with two tablespoons baking powder, stir all together, add teaspoon vanilla, bake in loaf or layers, make icing of melted chocolate cake, tablespoon butter, one-half cup brown sugar, cook; when cool spread on cake or use as filling.

Mexican Candy

Two cups dark brown sugar, one-half cup water, teaspoon butter, cook until it forms a soft ball in water, put pecan nuts in bottom of buttered saucers and pour sugar on while hot; let cool and there is the little thin round cakes one sees on the street sold by Mexicans.

A Type of Spanish Women

Another Type of Spanish Women

Mrs. Haffner-Ginger in her Kitchen

Mrs. Haffner-Ginger giving a Lesson in How to Set a Table

California audience watching Mrs. Haffner-Ginger make a Spanish Omelet

LIST OF MEXICAN SUPPLIES
IN MEXICAN STORES

As safron (Safron), used for flavoring meat and chile dishes.

Oregano (Mexican sage), used for flavoring all meat and chile dishes.

Cominos (common seed), used for flavoring all meat and chile dishes.

Cilantio (Cariandos seed), used for flavoring all meat and chile dishes.

Frijoles Colorado (pink beans).

Appelito Marado (a blue Mexican bean).

Belotas (Mexican acorns).

Pinones (pine nuts).

Maize Blanco (white corn), used for Mexican dishes.

Ojas (corn husk for Tamales).

Queso de tina (cheese made of cactus sweetened).

Queso Mexicano (a Mexican cheese).

Panocha (dark cane sugar in cone shape cakes).

Piloncillo (light brown cane sugar in cone shape cakes).

Chile Colorado (red chile), chile sauce.

Dule tipinos (small round red chile used for pepper sauces).

Pinole corn or wheat parched ground for Mexican drink, flavored with cinnamon and sweetened with sugar, mixed with milk or water.

Nixtamal Mexican Corn prepared old time way, ground in mortars.

Choriso (Mexican sausage).

Jammiello (Hamirello), candy made of pumpkin.

Cojeta de membrio, preserves made of quinces and Panocha.

Cojeta de camote, sweet potatoes and panocha, preserves.

Tamarindo, a dried fruit to soak in water and sweetened for a drink.

Tomatillas, a small wild green tomato.

Lector House believes that a society develops through a two-fold approach of continuous learning and adaptation, which is derived from the study of classic literary works spread across the historic timeline of literature records. Therefore, we aim at reviving, repairing and redeveloping all those inaccessible or damaged but historically as well as culturally important literature across subjects so that the future generations may have an opportunity to study and learn from past works to embark upon a journey of creating a better future.

This book is a result of an effort made by Lector House towards making a contribution to the preservation and repair of original ancient works which might hold historical significance to the approach of continuous learning across subjects.

HAPPY READING & LEARNING!

LECTOR HOUSE
LECTOR HOUSE LLP
E-MAIL: info@lectorhouse.com

9 789356 145757